Positive Thinking

A Pragmatic Workbook Designed To Cultivate A Positive Mindset By Effectively Training Your Inner Critic, Curbing Overthinking, And Transforming Your Overall Mindset

(The Key To Altering Your Mindset For Optimal Happiness)

Miodrag Reiner

Why You Shouldn't Handle Your Issues By Yourself: You're Not Alone.

Do you ever think that you'll never be able to get suitable rest because of your great abilities? That without you, everything would fall apart? Unfortunately, this kind of thinking causes a lot of people to become unhappy and overburdened with mounting problems.

When you're depressed and feeling overwhelmed by your issues, do you ever think, "No one in the world has ever experienced the same troubles as me"? This method of thinking is incorrect, despite the appearance that it is;

millions of people all over the world face the same problems.

The fact that there is hope at all times is wise. Let us imagine that some people have overcome "every imaginable terrible circumstance," and they persevered even in the face of overwhelming despair.

Conversely, negative thinking, pessimism, and solitude are more frequently the cause of sad and failed outcomes. You can combat this by reminding yourself to concentrate on the positive by taking steps toward optimistic beliefs.

In addition, our sense of importance can sometimes make us feel like we are carrying the entire weight of the world and its problems. However, your chances of coming up with a solution are diminished if you assume responsibility for every problem!

This results from the limited time we have to deal with issues that seem to have no end. Searching for answers leads to a lack of focus, anxiousness, and haste.

However, by practicing prayer or meditation, you can release this stress. You can also give tasks to others and organize yourself to achieve greater results and better health.

Knowing that you, your abilities, and your struggles are not wholly unique can help you accomplish more and live a happier life.

How life coaching can boost self-assurance and confidence

Life coaches are better equipped with methods and resources to assist you in growing your self-assurance and self-belief. Confidence coaching aims to help you start from the inside out by developing a positive view of life and boosting your self-image. You can develop a strong and positive self-image, question your beliefs, and increase your self-esteem with life coaching.

Recognize that people will believe in you if you do. A deeply ingrained sense of self-worth and confidence will make life more exciting, fulfilling, and enjoyable.

Self-assurance or self-belief

These two ideas represent your perceptions of your aptitudes, capacities, and conduct. A strong degree of self-confidence will enable you to pick things up quickly. Briefly, self-confidence is the ability to believe and trust in oneself. Furthermore, how we present ourselves to others is a key component of self-confidence.

Remember that we might project confidence on others without actually possessing it. Most people can present an outward front of assurance, but on the inside, they are shaking with terror! Many people use this tactic to hide low self-esteem that they would prefer no one else to know about.

Self-esteem or self-worth

These sum up how you feel about yourself, regardless of your appearance, accomplishments, or anything else you could be proud of. They are intimately linked to your level of self-respect and your ability to take pride in yourself. Being confident in your physical appearance and feeling good about yourself is a sign of having strong self-esteem.

How we view ourselves and others is correlated with our sense of self-worth. This includes various elements, including intelligence, beauty, prosperity, or value. The impact of poor self-esteem on mood can be profound. You can strive for perfection if you believe you are not worthy enough to feel you have accomplished enough.

When you have poor self-esteem or low self-worth, you could feel hopeless, unhappy, and guilty. You can even try to convince other people of your value. In addition, you might steer clear of potentially tense circumstances or difficulties you cannot handle.

Self-perception

This can be explained as a combination of confidence and self-worth. This idea includes your opinions about your appearance, aptitudes, age, accomplishments, and much more.

having self-assurance at work

This is an essential component of a successful career. In most professions, confidence is essential for day-to-day operations regardless of the circumstances. A strong feeling of self-worth can significantly influence your productivity and job satisfaction. It also has an impact on the way we speak with friends and coworkers.

When you are confident, you will be situationally aggressive, assertive, and focused at work. Being truly confident helps you make decisions that are beneficial to your home life and enable you to make a great influence at work. If you are experiencing difficulties with your confidence at work, a life coach can assist you in the following areas:

Coaching for leadership

Coaching for management

Mentoring in small businesses

settling disputes

Speaking in front of an audience

Controlling one's rage

control of stress

Executive mentorship

You may suffer from imposter syndrome if you lack confidence in yourself at work compared to other aspects of your life and don't think you deserve the success you've achieved.

The syndrome of impersonation

When you have this condition, you cannot absorb anything you achieve. Even when there is unquestionable evidence that your achievements are the product of skill and hard work, you could be plagued by a persistent sense of inadequacy. You might also experience intense self-doubt and feelings of intellectual fraudulence.

Though they can take many different forms, imposter feelings typically fall into the following categories:

Sensations of being untrue

You may have deceived people into believing you are more capable than you are. Furthermore, you can believe that your success and professional standing are unworthy of you. This is coupled with the anxiety of being found out. Statements such as these might be used to describe this type of feeling: * "I fear the day when my coworkers will realize how ignorant I am in the field. "I generally think I am more competent than I am."

You constantly blame luck for your achievements.

You can be prone to believing that your achievements result from chance or other outside forces rather than your abilities and tenacity. You can be recognized by the following statements: * "This was a fluke," * "I always get lucky," * and "This will not take place again."

Playing down achievement

When you accomplish anything for which others commend you, you will typically minimize your accomplishments. It will seem as though anyone might have achieved the feat.

You can relate to the following statements: * "It's not something big"; * "It wasn't of much importance"; * "I did well because it was easy."

If you think you may be suffering from this syndrome, you can start making changes in your life.

Methods of Imprinting

Deciding to alter one's behavior, mindset, or circumstances does not guarantee that the intended outcome will materialize. Deciding to change is just the first step in the process.

We now know your mental image of your desire is your objective. The objective becomes an intention when it is put in writing. "Imprinting" is the intentional control of our ideas and images on the changes we wish to achieve. It is the act of programming your subconscious to bring forth your intention. When our subconscious mind accepts the finished product's new image, imprinting occurs. Three steps make up the imprinting process:

You make a declaration of purpose to confirm your objective.

You visualize the outcome.

You experience the feeling that accompanies reaching the objective.

Let's go over each stage so that we fully understand the process.

Step 1: Use an "Intention Statement" to Affirm Your Objective.

Simply put, an "intention statement" is a factual or belief declaration expressed in the present tense, in a positive and personable style, as if the objective had already been accomplished.

An "intention statement" declares a particular want: "This is what I choose to be, do, or have."

By focusing the mental image on the desired outcome, you can consciously manipulate your subconscious's programming when you write down your objectives.

Step 2: Visualize the Final Outcome

Imagine and feel in your mind's eye the realization of the desired outcome. Envision oneself as a vital participant in the achievement. Constructive "synthetic visualization," sometimes known as "virtual reality," is based on the displacement hypothesis. You are replacing your outdated image of yourself and your old photo with a fresh one. Recall that we shall advance toward the imagined objective.

Step 3 is to Experience the Feeling of Success.

Feelings have a stronger effect on the subconscious than words do. Positive emotions have no greater effect on it than negative ones. It only reacts to emotions. Feelings and emotions are crucial for effect since the more we can attach to a concept, the quicker it will materialize. It might be argued that the frequency with which we employ envisioning and emotional involvement will directly correlate with the manifestation of our desire. You should visualize yourself achieving the desired outcome and experiencing the delight and fulfillment that comes with it.

For imprinting to be successful, all three processes are required. About ten percent of attempts to read or express your intentions will be successful. You will have roughly a 55% success rate if you clearly explain your aims and visualize the outcome. Expect a 100 o/o success rate if you read or articulate your objectives, visualize the outcome, and experience the emotion associated with realizing what you envision!

The Influence of Goals

In Chapter 6, we had a quick discussion regarding affirmations. Affirmations and intentions are comparable. Because they are intended to achieve a particular outcome, they are slightly more targeted than affirmations.

Why do intentions have such power? Simply put, the mind becomes conditioned to perceive things differently when a goal or notion is repeatedly repeated, especially when combined with emotion. Eventually, the intention gets ingrained in your mind as a constant thought. Our intentions are the key to altering our reality since our ideas consistently create our reality.

Are Intentional Statements Effective?

Maybe you're one of those people who think intention statements are useless, or maybe you think that while intention statements are a nice idea in theory, they fall short of expectations in practice.

Many individuals give intention statements a try and then give them up. "I tried using intention statements, and they don't work!" is a common statement I hear from folks. But in actuality, they function. They are incredibly dependable and do draw affirmation into people's lives.

Here are several reasons why intention statements don't seem to work if you haven't had any luck utilizing them. Please pay attention to this as it is very crucial. The sole reason intention statements don't seem to work is that an aspect of the invention process isn't fully understood. It is related to what is genuinely confirmed.

The purpose is not the issue. We have hard evidence that intention statements are effective if we pay attention to the self-talk we tell ourselves. We constantly express our intentions about the attitudes and beliefs we now hold in our daily conversations and our self-talk. We have arrived at our current location thanks to these intention expressions. They have prevented us from getting what we desire or enabled us to create what we desire.

Making sure the actual intention statements that are having an impact are the ones we want is necessary to fully utilize the power of intention statements. That presents our main obstacle.

Regretfully, most people who use intention statements don't succeed in their endeavors. Why? Because they are lying to themselves when they say that's what they intend to do! They are still lying to themselves, however unintentionally. Their stated objective differs from the "true" intention.

In actuality, what's occurring is that their goal statement and their true beliefs are at odds; thus, when they express their intention, a powerful but subdued competing intention is typically appended at the end. I refer to these conflicting goals as "Nega-Tags."

For instance, if you say, "I want to lose weight," one or more Nega-Tags will probably appear after your intention statement. They may proceed as follows:

"Others will expect me to keep the weight off if I lose it."

Men will come up to me and ask for sex if I lose weight. "

"I'll have to give up my favorite foods if I lose the weight. "

"I will need to spend a lot of money on new clothes if I lose weight. "

There is an infinite number of Nega-Tags. Naturally, they are not spoken or articulated but subtly (and effectively) reflect the current barriers to achieving your goals.

3.

Muting the Distraction: The Technique of Positive Self-Talk

P

Imagine traveling up a mountain and negotiating the icy cliffs to reach the summit. Your inner voice is a continuous friend offering guidance and/or criticism. How might having that partner alter your assessment of your uphill journey's success? This chapter focuses on changing that voice from criticism to encouragement, a helpful friend who inspires you to meet life's obstacles head-on with fortitude and hope. She's a great companion to have! That is the main goal of using constructive self-talk. It's the skill of substituting inspiring, uplifting ideas with a harsh, judgmental inner monologue. Suggests that talking to oneself positively boosts motivation and self-esteem.

Recall that the key is recognizing the opportunity for growth in life's obstacles rather than ignoring reality. Prominent life coach Tony Robbins once quipped, "The only thing standing between you and your goals is the story you keep telling yourself." Positive self-talk may transform our approach to life by reducing stress and promoting optimism.

First, learn to identify negative internal chatter. It frequently contains phrases like "can't," "won't," and "shouldn't." Question these ideas, then rephrase them. Practice this change every day. For example, utilize the time to do something fun, like flipping through the radio stations until you locate a song you enjoy, rather than worrying about being trapped in traffic. Then give it your all-out vocal performance! Alternatively, think to yourself in a lengthy checkout line, "Man, I'm glad I don't have a migraine right now! I feel very well. I feel very fortunate to be in such good health today! Practice indeed makes perfect for this skill.

Positive Self-Talk with Powerful Words: Affirmations

Similar to individualized mantras, affirmations are uplifting, empowering declarations that support constructive self-talk. Motivating writer Louise Hay once said, "Every thought we think is creating our future." Create affirmations that are present-tense, uplifting, and personal. Make frequent use of them, maybe with the help of smartphone apps like ThinkUp or sticky notes. Demonstrated the practical advantages of positive self-talk by showing how affirmations improve problem-solving under pressure. Like a domino effect, regular practice can dramatically increase confidence and self-esteem.

Saying kind words to yourself isn't the goal of positive self-talk; rather, it's about making positive decisions more frequently. This exercise enhances your relationships with other people as well as with yourself. Positive self-talk has been demonstrated by University of Texas researchers to enhance interpersonal connections. Being grounded, at ease, and peaceful radiates positivity into your interactions. It spreads easily! Similar to how a negative attitude may spread. Good vibes multiply.

As Oprah famously remarked, "A person can change their future by merely changing their attitude, which is the greatest discovery of all time." It's about tuning out the negative and tuning in to a frequency of hope, encouragement, and resilience. Remember that your inner voice can be your most powerful ally as we continue.

Section Two

The Science of Wealth Creation

Franklin expands on the Science of Getting Rich concept in this chapter. He points out that this science is a romantic ideology and a realistic and useful method of creating money. He makes the case that anyone may succeed similarly by adhering to the same principles and offers instances of successful people who have done so.

Reiterating that there is a science to becoming wealthy and that this science is founded on Frankie's starts. He contends that the same rules of nature that regulate the material world also govern the mental and spiritual domains, and these laws are those of wealth creation:

"There is a science of getting rich; a person.

According to Frankie, the rules of wealth creation can be discovered via self-education and observation, even though they are not taught in schools or universities. He encourages readers to pursue the information and tools required to become wealthy and assume complete responsibility for their financial future.

Natural Laws for Generating Wealth

Frankie continues by outlining a few of the inherent principles of generating riches. He underlines that these rules are objective, universal, and applicable to everybody who chooses to use them—rather than arbitrary or subjective:

"Any person who possesses a certain set of talents and abilities, who adheres to certain mental laws and who takes a certain course of action, can become rich with mathematical certainty."

Frankie argues that causes and consequences, rather than chance or luck, are the foundation of the laws of wealth generation. He says that one can generate the causes that will result in the desired effects—wealth and abundance—by comprehending these basic principles.

The Appropriate Mental Frame

According to Frankie, possessing the appropriate mindset is one of the fundamental principles of wealth development. He contends that the main factors influencing a person's ability to succeed financially are their attitudes and beliefs:

"Having the right attitude towards wealth is the first step towards acquiring it. If you think negatively about wealth, you will never achieve it. On the other hand, if you think positively about wealth, it will soon come to you."

He contends that to attract riches, one must have an optimistic and bountiful mindset. He highlights the significance of believing in oneself to be able to accomplish one's goals and of seeing oneself as already wealthy and successful.

The Rule of Appreciation

Frankie says there's another natural law of wealth creation: the law of gratitude. He contends that instead of dwelling on one's shortcomings, one should learn to be grateful for what one currently has:

"Gr Frankie's attitude is one of the most powerful emotions for creating wealth. It is a magnet for the good things in life. By being grateful for what you have, you also attract more of what you want."

Argues that to attract more wealth, one must learn to value and appreciate what they already have, no matter how modest or little. He highlights that cultivating an attitude of thankfulness is a habit that can be achieved via repetition and practice.

The Value of Taking Action

As she closes the chapter, Frankie emphasizes the value of moving toward one's goals. He contends that intentional and consistent action cannot be replaced by positive thinking or visualization:

"Thinking and visualizing are important, but they are not enough. Unless you take action towards your goals, nothing will happen. The key to wealth creation is to take purposeful and consistent action, no matter how small."

Frankie contends that rather than anticipating quick fixes and spectacular outcomes, one should concentrate on making tiny, gradual progress toward their objectives. He highlights that perseverance and focus are disappointments and that success is a process rather than an event.

The Grand Entrance

Hi to all of you!

Jackson James is my name.

I will be your positivity mentor and traveling partner on this amazing adventure to discover the more positive version of yourself. Yes, you have a more positive self, and despite what you may believe, I can assure you that it is very much alive and well. Sometimes, though, it gets lost under all the junk life throws at us.

Together, we shall explore a place where the extraordinary becomes routine daily, and the force of positivity is unrestricted. A location where those who haven't yet joined us on this incredible journey will stand on life's sidewalk, stunned and in awe of how the transformed you will approach everything with unwavering optimism, drive, and success resolve. And they will never know what happened to their friend, coworker, or loved one until they come on this journey with us. Yes, it will be amazing, yes, it will be insane, and yes, it will permanently alter your life.

This is a truth.

You have a large brain!

I am not referring only to the physical dimensions here, even if they have tripled in size during our evolutionary history. No, its computeable size is what I mean. There are 86 billion neurons; each crammed into a space smaller than a sardine can within your head. These neurons are linked to thousands of other neurons, resulting in trillions of synaptic connections. It can hold 2.5 petabytes of data in storage. I had no idea what a petabyte was either, but it turns out that it's roughly the same as watching three million hours of Don, Poppy, and Kaitlin's morning program. Not something you want to do! It is large and extremely fast, able to move all that data inside there more quickly than a helicopter on a fast track. Furthermore, did you know that your brain generates enough electricity to light a lightbulb physically? What a great idea that is!

Why am I saying all of this to you?

That's to let you know how extraordinarily fortunate we are as a species to hold more than 100,000 MacBook Pros in our minds without losing our balance. It seems terrible that after being blessed with such a wonderful technological advancement, we let it lapse into negativity and complain about things like the rain being too wet, the grass being the incorrect shade of green, or the lack of heat in our lattes. Imagine a world where we focused our energies on the positive aspects of our life, conquering negativity in a single 'Super-sized' bond, and didn't mind if the lawn wasn't mowed that week or if our name wasn't spelled correctly on the side of the coffee we were holding. Imagine the opportunities that might arise for leisure, work, and home. Imagine a society without taxes or speeding fines since the human mind would be adept at making wise choices, triumphing over hardship, and improving the planet. Well, that is the path we are about to take, my positivity searchers. Despite your dread, Tax Inspectors, proceed.

Since nobody enjoys traveling with strangers, let me take this opportunity to properly introduce myself before our excursion.

Yes, my name sounds backward. My name is Jackson James. I'm grateful, Dad and Mom. Josephine is my sister's name. I believe I would have liked that. She never seemed to voice complaints.

I grew up in London, where I was born. That's London, England, not London Island, Ontario, Arkansas, or any other twenty-six other make-believe Londons that exist just to confuse. None of which have our black cabs, red buses, or an environment full of pollutants to gnaw on.

To my father's joy, I completed my education at Cambridge very well. However, to his dismay, I chose to travel instead of getting a real career. I traveled the world, living in Europe before we rejected them, Asia before we mistrusted them, and America before we disagreed with the political establishment. I have worked for some of the biggest companies over the years, applying my extensive knowledge of psychology and human interaction to help them use the potential of their frequently alienated workforce by modifying their efforts to best suit the company's needs. This introduced me to the wonderful discipline of "Positive Psychology," which I utilized to even greater effect by reorganizing these companies to center around their workforce. I've moved to the San Francisco Bay Area and love the wine bars, cafes, and lattes with my name written backward.

Why does this matter? My agent has informed me with great confidence that the initial phase of the book, during which we get to know one another, is crucial. During this time, we form a bond, and you guys conclude that I'm the person you should trust with any advice regarding the subject matter featured on the front cover—in this case, positive thinking. To further cement this as a Unibond moment, let me assure you that everything I suggest in this book is supported by evidence. It functions. True to the fullest extent! I thank my lucky stars that no one else has dared to put it all down and publish it before me. I have been using it for many years in various countries throughout the world and urging others to do the same for equally as many years.

Another crucial point to remember is that this book does not contain copied ideas that have been misspelled or written using different terms. There is something novel and inventive in store for us. Activities and information transfers shift your internal thermometer from a cold, negative state to a sunny, warm state by altering your thoughts.

The intended readership of this work is a crucial topic to discuss. According to popular belief, when writing a book, you should first focus on writing for a specific niche, like business owners who wear high heels, to make your book resonate and magically soar to the top of the best-seller list for that specific group of business owners who wear excessively tight shoes. Now, much to my agent's dismay—and with the real chance that she'll point a bony finger at me later and say, "I told you so"—I have completely ignored this advice. I apologize for the conventional knowledge! Perhaps the next time.

This book is especially addressed to all of you. I understand it may seem a little contradictory, but bear with me. Despite having many business scenarios, it's not only for business. Even though it contains a number of those examples, it is not only for private usage. This book is meant for all ages and both living and deceased people. I have carefully prepared these tactics here, and there is no reason why you cannot utilize them at any moment in your life or the hereafter. The good news is that you can transform your entire life most beneficially by putting this system of strategies into practice (pardon the pun). The ' many people' who wish to refocus their minds to reflect the power of positive thinking for their lifetime success are the target audience for this book.

Before we begin, there is one more thing to discuss. I adore well-written grammar. I appreciate it, and reading a book with proper spelling and punctuation is enjoyable. That book is not this one. I apologize to the rival grammar enthusiasts among you. I have disregarded some rules and guidelines associated with producing a well-edited and grammatically sound book because I'm going to be talking to you, and I don't talk like that. For example, I frequently begin sentences with Andand many Buts. I tried to follow the rules, but I don't think you'll talk that way either, so please don't judge me if you're a grammar expert.

Now, I purposefully omitted any mention of the difficult times I faced in my introductory introduction. You know, those difficult times in life when you find yourself heading down a path that ultimately leads to really gloomy places. Furthermore, I'm not merely referring to Dagenham here. I mean, these are very gloomy times. After watching an episode of Plane Crash Investigates, there are moments that you would prefer to forget but, regrettably, can't seem to get rid of. But the one thing that has always got me through those difficult moments is people. You probably assumed that I would respond with "positive thinking." Well, maybe a close second, but as far as I've discovered in my 42 orbits around the sun, people are what make a difference in life. That includes everyone traveling with us and beyond, including you and me.

Individuals do matter, but not always in a bad way, and when they do, it's usually for the wrong reasons. Keep traffic wardens in mind. When was the last time you truly needed assistance and reached out to someone? I refer to a circumstance in which you were forced to seek an ally and enlist their help. Did you get in touch with someone who was genuinely helpful? Was that person's temperament favorable or unfavorable?

They were probably of the former. You are aware of the individuals I refer to. Those who refuse to let life's negative stand in their way. The men and women of this planet who, to those who know them well, discreetly murmur, 'I have your back; you can count on me,' possess a unique magical aura. I mean, those are the people we will be; those are the people I mean.

ManageingUnfavorable Thoughts

I now understand that I prolonged all of my life's unpleasant and difficult periods by dwelling too much on my thoughts. I was thinking about past mistakes, lost opportunities, and other instances that left me disappointed and angry or wondering about the future. I had no idea how much my life was affected by negative beliefs.

According to scientific studies, an individual's mind contains between 60,000 and 70,000 thoughts daily, of which 95% are useless or bad. The daily struggles I was facing not only took away from my ability to appreciate life's pleasures but also sapped my energy and diverted my attention from what mattered in my life.

This chapter will teach you the causes of your negative thoughts and strategies for overcoming them.

What makes one think negatively? Finding the why—what sets off your negative thinking—should be your first step. Negative thinking can influence your life if you can figure out why you are thinking negatively so much of the time.

Disorders of the Mind. There are numerous reasons for negative thoughts, and each person may have a different cause. Mental health disorders, including anxiety disorder (GAD) and obsessive-compulsive disorder (OCD), can be the biggest contributors to negative thinking.

Negative thoughts can also be attributed to depression. To receive medical advice if you believe you may be suffering from a mental illness, get in touch with a mental health specialist.

Thinking back. Everyone occasionally thinks negatively; feeling depressed or unhappy is a normal aspect of life. The risk for us is when these unfavorable ideas keep coming back to us.

Scholars refer to the phenomenon as ruminating. Rumination is a habit that can be detrimental to our mental health since it can exacerbate or prolong depression and make it more difficult for us to think clearly and regulate our feelings.

The impact of cortisol. One of the hormones that our bodies use extensively and that is mostly released during times of stress is cortisol. Human health depends on maintaining the proper cortisol balance, and issues might arise if your adrenal gland releases too little or too much cortisol.

Because cortisol alerts us to impending danger, our brain is fascinated. The issue arises when we regularly subject our bodies and thoughts to high levels of stress and negative thinking, which leads to an excess of cortisol in the body. Negative thought patterns become ingrained in our brains and become normal.

We program our minds to believe that we are safe and that this is our new normal while our cortisol levels rise dangerously. The body will eventually exhibit indicators of aging, such as heart attacks, anxiety, depression, and mental illness.

Should you fail to manage your pessimistic thoughts, you will ultimately have to deal with severe health problems.

Clinging to regrets and worries. Within the scientific world, American psychologist, educator, and self-help book author Martin Seligman is well-known for his beliefs on positive psychology and well-being. According to him, the three main reasons why most individuals have negative thoughts are:

Apprehension about the future. Believe that the worst things, like failure or disaster, are inevitable. People who fear the future are diverted from living in the now, where they have greater control over their lives because the future hasn't happened yet.

Worry about the here and now. Many of us are concerned with what other people think of us, how traffic will be on our way home, or whether we perform well at work. We are more prone to negative thoughts when we are in a toxic relationship or situation.

Feel regret over the past. Everybody commits acts for which they feel guilty or uncomfortable. Negative thinkers tend to focus more than others on their previous transgressions and shortcomings.

You can control negative thoughts using certain tactics, regardless of what triggers them. As soon as you realize your negative thoughts will become a major issue in your life, you must address them.

The Craft of Innovative Visualisation

Vibrant, swirling tapestries of our wants grace the walls of the magnificent gallery that is our imagination. The enchanted process of creative visualization is used to make this artwork. We may create vivid mental images that bring our dreams to life, much like skilled painters, into the realm of creative imagination and how important it is to realize our goals.

The Imagination Canvas

There is an infinite space in the enormous geography of our brains that we call the universe. This is the hallowed place where visions come to life, the commonplace transforms into the spectacular, and our creative spirit reaches its greatest heights.

Imagination is the alchemical furnace in which ideas become works of art, and the ordinary is elevated to the sublime. Traveling beyond the known and into the realm of the extraordinary is an adventure through a land of boundless possibilities.

The power of the Canvas of Imagination is limitless; it cuts over boundaries and cultural contexts. The common tongue links all people, recognizing that our creative sources are the same. Our diversity is the vivid canvas on which we create our group's masterpiece.

The compass that leads us across the unexplored territory of the unknown is the Canvas of Imagination. It serves as a reminder that our dreams are the paintbrushes and our imaginations the brushes with which we paint the world. We can reshape and mold our reality.

Let's embrace the limitless canvas of our imagination and acknowledge that we are always painting the world in the vivid hues of our fantasies. Let our creative spirit serve as our compass as we explore the horizons of infinite possibilities and elevate the commonplace to the extraordinary. On this voyage, we discover not just our imagination but also the rich, dynamic details of our existence.

Increasing the Force of Attraction

The Law of Attraction, which holds that like attracts like, is closely related to creative visualization. We radiate a frequency that attracts our wants into our lives when we have a clear and positive picture of what we want.

The Law of Attraction is an unwritten contract between our thoughts and the universe that applies to everything. It suggests that the energy we release from our aspirations, beliefs, and intentions will magnetically draw like energy from the cosmos. Similar to how each instrument in a symphony plays a certain part, our thoughts also contribute to the intricate arrangement of our lives.

The tune that follows us everywhere we go is the Law of Attraction. It is the conductor of our aspirations and the arranger of our possibilities. We become the protagonists of our tales, the masters of our fates, and the carriers of limitless creative potential by magnifying this law.

Jim Carrey

Amid the sparkling lights and stars of Hollywood, amid the wide-open spaces, an artist who goes beyond entertainment to become a symbol of inspiration lives. What's his name? Jim Carrell. a real transformational master.

Jim Carrey is more than just an actor—he is a shape-shifter, a character creator, and a versatility virtuoso. He embodies artistic fluidity and can play various characters with a chameleon-like appearance. But underneath the paint and masks, there's a tale of adversity, tenacity, and persistent dream-chasing.

Carrey's route, which brought him into the maze of Hollywood and exposed him to the shadows of rejection and the mist of uncertainty, is comparable to that of the hero. Like many heroes, though, he persevered because of his unrelenting will to succeed and his unshakeable faith in his abilities.

Jim Carrey has ventured into the domain of inspiration, surpassing humor and entertainment. His experience is proof of the strength of belief. Before becoming well-known, he drew himself a 10 million dollar cheque for "acting services rendered," he kept it as a reminder of his steadfast faith in his aspirations. Surprisingly, fate agreed with his steadfast belief because he later received that exact amount for his performance in "Dumb and Dumber."

Jim Carrey's impact is seen in the field of transformative wisdom, far beyond his cinematic roles. He talks about how important it is to embrace the limitless possibilities of love and creativity and live a life free from the restrictions of fear. Many people have found great resonance in his inspiring lectures, which remind us that our thoughts can influence our fate.

The story of Jim Carrey is a beacon of wisdom. It encourages us to believe in the boundless potential inside of us and to fervently and unwaveringly follow our aspirations. He is a living example of how we can turn our lives into inspirational masterpieces with faith, perseverance, and humor.

Jim is a shimmering reminder that we can change, create, and inspire. His story inspires us to accept our metamorphoses and become the architects of our destinies since it is a perfect example of the hero that each of us possesses.

Chapter 2: Thinking Too Much

Overanalyzing is a prevalent issue that leads to anxiety and poor health. Moreover, using positive thinking practices is impeded by overthinking. This chapter defines overthinking and discusses potential consequences.

What does it mean to overthink something?

The Buddhist doctrine provides a fantastic parallel for the suffering many of us experience from constant, concentrated thought. This continual flipping between ideas is referred to as "monkey mind." Buddha explained it thus way:

This metaphor, called kapicitta in Buddhist teaching, encapsulates how many of us respond to stress and a constant barrage of information. We are easily sidetracked and can't concentrate on one thing at a time.

We notice that you cannot come to a conclusion and are always jumping from one troubling idea to the next. We obsess about the past, particularly the things we think went wrong. We focus on the future, planning our activities for the upcoming day, week, or month. Ultimately, we are not focused enough on what we are currently doing.

Insomnia is also linked to the monkey mind. When we lie down and close our eyes, our minds race rather than bring us rest and tranquility. Our minds race with ideas, which makes us anxious and prevents us from falling asleep. According to the Buddha's teachings, the monkey mind has plagued humans for countless millennia. But having a monkey mind is even more typical in today's environment, where a million things are vying for our attention. Positive thinking is thwarted by monkey mentality. Your mind will never be still if it is always racing with ideas. Finding calmness in concentration and learning to quiet the monkey mind are two strategies used in positive thinking.

In psychology, we refer to overthinking as the monkey mind. Uncontrollable or bothersome thoughts that keep you from concentrating on anything are a symptom of this mind pattern. It is frequently linked to compulsive thoughts about the past or hypothetical future events. It frequently centers on what you could have done differently for a better result. It is utterly fruitless to keep repeating past incidents or attempting to forecast possible outcomes for the future. The past is not something you can alter. It is restricted to what you can do to influence the future. Instead, you must develop the ability to give the present moment your attention and energy.

When an issue with overthinking arises

We all overanalyze to some extent. With so many conflicting demands on our time and attention, the modern world may be chaotic. It is a rare person who can maintain composure under these circumstances. Most people experience intermittent sleep problems.

They frequently do this due to worrying about the past or the future.

It turns into a significant issue when overthinking persists and negatively impacts you over time. Chronic overthinking affects how you react to others and makes it challenging to manage your daily life efficiently. When you overthink anything, you become anxious, worn out, and fixated on unfavorable ideas such as "Did I say the right thing?" "Will I appear foolish at tomorrow's meeting?"

Overthinking can develop into a disease that can interfere with everything you do if you just can't get things done because you are frightened of failing or making the same mistakes again or if you find it difficult to concentrate on what you are doing because you are thinking about the past or the future. It is linked to depression and obsessive-compulsive disorder, and it can cause anxiety and stress.

Are you overthinking things all the time?

The Spoon Isn't Real.

To what extent is our world true? To what extent is the information we are told by commercial knowledge true? Would you believe me if I told you that humans are aimless wanderers with no control over their lives? Throughout our lives, someone else makes decisions on our behalf. The only thing that gives us any sense of inner calm is the false sense of choice placed before us. Thousands of lost souls pass each other on the streets every day, oblivious to the fact that they are traveling in circles. Everybody feels special and important, or at least they ought to. However, how do we interpret this? How can we articulate it? How do we make sense of the things we think and do? How do we resolve internal problems inside ourselves? How do we quiet the voices that don't always appear to belong to us? The universal education system forces us to embrace paradigms that shape our perception of reality, which is the source of human feelings of shame and terror. The way the world seems is not real. If it did, the sun's life-giving rays would penetrate and envelop us in darkness. To see that our common goal in this life is self-fulfillment, we must discover the light within.

No matter where I begin, almost every route will eventually realize that everything we know has been purposefully altered. Deciding what to believe and what not to believe in life is challenging. So, when we first embark on our trip together, I advise having complete faith in fairy tales. In this modest but, in my view, intriguing tale, we shall discuss knowing rather than belief. You may think Santa Claus exists, but how much good has it done us? We were duped from the start because time has proven that we must personally put the gifts under the Christmas tree. Our family tricks us from the moment we are born, telling us that if we behave well, a red-riding reindeer will come and bestow upon us a priceless present.

Is that really how life is meant to be? Given that we begin with conviction in a living lie, what happens next? And it gets worse from there. Our parents instill in us early on the belief that lying is a desirable habit or a program. This is passed down to us by our parents, who themselves got this questionable gift from their parents, who got it from theirs. Alright, so it's not a serious crime, but even at birth, you can see that life may not be all that colorful—at least not in a moral sense. I mean, we could have made a day just for loved ones to give and receive gifts to show each other how much they care. What is in its place? Present-giving is a ritual that we engage in, but it's important to note that the reason behind it all isn't love—rather, it's a belief that the "first star" fell twenty centuries ago. That one deceit conceals another is a concept we are all familiar with. It appears that life will continue in this manner forever, or even until the end.

Individuals are taught that, in certain cases, their destiny is not in their hands and instead depends on a higher power—or, in more practical terms, a few masked thugs who openly lie on television while posing as honest people. Well, the outcome couldn't have been much better. What follows then? It turns into a lottery where your birth predetermines your life path. Chaos, lack of control—just a frantic pursuit of fame and fortune. In theory, you would worry less now if born into a wealthy household. You start somewhat less pleasantly if your family is poorer. Naturally, happiness is a function of circumstances; wealth is not a gauge of it. That being said, many who lack wealth tend to use this as an excuse for their circumstances. Because the truth is you need money, not just a little bit of it, if you want to live on the fringe, slaughtering moose and fishing in the backcountry. This book is adapted to harsh, raw realities where life might sometimes appear ruthless. This is the world in which we live.

But is life truly so cruel? It appears out of nowhere that someone has been harmed by life. So what, when things go wrong, is life to blame?

Depending on one's beliefs, assigning responsibility for one's fate to a certain deity is best. People are so carefully prepared by the government system from birth that they find it harder and harder to solve their problems as they age. A person is extremely independent from birth until they start picking up on the words their carers are using. After the child grows up, the caregivers—whom the system has conditioned to do so—start stifling their children's independence and forcing the same patterns into their minds that they were raised with. A seemingly never-ending vicious loop is thus initiated. People lose independence as they become older and mistakenly think everything is colorful.

Adults and adolescents frequently fail to recognize their issues at first. But one day, out of nowhere, these issues pile up one after the other as life progresses. There comes a point in life for most people—perhaps not for everyone—but it's difficult to avoid meeting someone who has gone through a breakdown. Everybody has problems of one kind or another. It can happen that we don't get the help we need, and the entire world is insulted.

Yes, this is not how our lives should appear. Constantly losing control and chasing after aspirations that never seem to come true. When you overcome one challenge, another appears on the same path. As they say, what doesn't kill us makes us stronger. But one day, an issue arises for which there doesn't appear to be a fix. What happens next? The most depressing thing is that, up until they go through a challenging or even life-changing event, people just follow the path their carers and the government system have taught them without questioning anything around them. At that point, they start to look for answers and alternative solutions to the problems.

The fact that individuals frequently consider themselves to be unimportant beings is incredibly cruel and ugly. They hurt themselves, for starters, and it's bad for humanity as a whole. Even though most people can't imagine the possibilities in our carefully designed reality, most people glance about and frequently don't realize what they're looking at. Life eludes us, time flies, and it's not a pretty picture when we look back. What action could I have taken? What could I have done differently? It's best not to consider the latter. What could I have done better? Time goes on, the colors have long since faded, the greyness gets deeper, and it appears that nothing more can be done. Ten, twenty, or thirty years ago, dreams are still dreams. The children visit once a year for the holidays and phone on birthdays, but the spouse has long since stopped communicating because there is nothing to discuss. That's life, I suppose.

After all, what can we do? In addition to the political and economic system, there are scientists, technologies, and the infinite and unfathomable cosmic universe in which we are but specks. Simply said, we are common people who have been led to feel that "it's their big fault." It doesn't appear overly optimistic, as I stated at the outset. Even if it's not their aim, our carers lie to us from the moment we are born. Then, it is determined by the hat you were born wearing. Greetings and welcome to the game "Life."

Or maybe it's completely different; maybe people have been persuaded— directly or indirectly—that they are unimportant because someone is interested in that. Why not follow the theory that everyone has their own evil goal, as life starts with a lie? If we can break these patterns, perhaps we can explain this deficiency in civilizational reasoning from other angles. The world has two dominant forces: "thinking" and "not thinking." Once you go through one door, you can see the top from the threshold. It's reachable via a lovely, well-marked path, although it does require some thought. As you go through the other door, you won't know where to look. Thick fog will envelop the top as the path winds through a twisting, dark woodland. Which way do you wish to go? Which door would you rather open? One that ends in nothing or will leave you feeling incredibly fulfilled? Do you want to experience regret for yourself, the people in your life, and your surroundings? Alternatively, would you rather experience joy and contentment and wish for time to stop so that you might declare, "This is the moment I've been waiting for"? You can choose two pathways in life: the path to the top and the path to nothingness. You will experience inner delight and fulfillment at the top and realize that your life has a purpose. All of a sudden, you will realize that there can be many summits like this one.

The alternative route will deprive you of everything, extinguish your vital force, and lead you into the pitfalls of apathy. Every second you waste, you'll regret it. What's the funniest of all, you ask? Time cannot be turned back, so all that's left is a hallucinogenic laugh that will make your tears seem justified. Take time to reflect on the route you have chosen for yourself. What kind of life do you wish to provide the people closest to you and yourself? Everything that occurs in your life affects everyone around you and yourself. In this small group game, players assume personal responsibility while directly influencing everyone around them.

It's Critical What We Say While Tapping!

I would want to talk about a few more features of tapping before explaining how and why it functions. The tapping statement is one facet.

We tested with various tapping statements during our Discovery Evening and identified the most successful ones.

The comments we make while tapping are crucial.

Our subconscious minds are preprogrammed with all of our notions. Subconsciously, we have to erase unhealthy feelings and beliefs if we want to make changes in our lives. The comments we make when tapping serve as instructions to the subconscious mind, and they must be made in a way that eliminates any negative feelings or beliefs.

For instance, You board a cab. You are still not at your destination several hours later. You wonder, "Why?" because you failed to tell the cab driver where you were going!

It's like hailing a cab without telling the driver where we're going if we just tap without providing a sufficient tapping remark!

Two Crucial Elements of the Tapping Declaration

1. The best statements to tap into are those that support the dysfunctional belief that is held at the moment.

We risk undermining the tapping process by forgetting the message or being distracted by other things if the remark we verbalize while tapping conflicts with the dysfunctional belief we now hold.

For instance, you don't feel in control. You feel like a loser, a wimp, and a coward. The body will remind you that you are weak and that you are not just weak but also a wimp, a coward, and a loser if the tapping phrase is "I am empowered." Alternatively, if we tap "I am not powerful," this statement aligns with the dysfunctional belief that is currently held.

An EFT Tapping statement that supports the prevailing opinion is less likely to be tampered with by the body.

One of the clients stopped tapping in the middle of the Discovery Evening and said, "It's raining outside." It had poured rain the entire day. It was not a sudden downpour. The downpour completely diverted this tapper's attention. After some laughter, the group had a conversation. We found that for the tapping statement to be effective, it had to align with the problematic belief, memory, or feeling that was currently present.

Our bodies are meant to protect us, whether healthy or unhealthy. If we were to tap on the thought that we are powerful instead of believing we are weak, our body would recognize that this is untrue and might interfere with or divert our attention from the tapping. If the EFT Tapping statement is consistent with the prevailing belief, the body is less likely to undermine the tapping and the procedure.

2. Tapping statements and the subconscious mind

The center half of the tapping statements contains directives for the subconscious. We just give a damn about what our subconscious hears when we tap. I appreciate these three rules of the subconscious mind. "The three P Rules."

The Subconscious Mind Follows Three Rules:

1. Personal. It can only comprehend "I," "me," and "myself." In the first person.

2. Favourable. The word "no" is not heard by the subconscious. The subconscious interprets statements like "I am not going to eat that piece of cake" as "Yummm! Cake! I am going to eat a piece of that cake!"

3. The current moment. The subconscious does not understand time. It is exclusively aware of "now," or the present. "Tomorrow, I am going to clean the garage." Because tomorrow never comes, we put off cleaning the garage.

At the Discovery Evening, we experimented with several kinds of tapping statements. Many of my customers reported that their minds wandered and became so engrossed while tapping "I am powerful" that they forgot what they were tapping.

There were a lot of yawns when we added the word "not" to the basic statement, "I am not powerful." The body lets you know when a tapping statement is cleared by yawning. We got amazing results when we continued with more statements and ended each with a "no" or "not."

When someone says, "I am not powerful," the physical body is soothed by the "not," and the subconscious is told, "I am powerful!" My clients now only want to tap sentences containing "no" or "not." They consider it clever to touch statements that end in "no" or "not." I concur.

Section Three

The Subtle Art of Belief in Oneself

Self-assurance is a powerful quality. Something starts to happen as soon as you begin to believe in yourself. Though it takes a lot of work, changing our thoughts eventually pays off. It would be like operating a vehicle with the handbrakes on if you were to operate in any way without the requisite self-beliefs. A great deal of energy is squandered as a result.

Your beliefs should not hold you back but should propel you forward. Half the battle won't be lost when you feel you can. You will likely succeed in the real world once you have triumphed over the mental war.

Now, we'll go over what beliefs are, why they matter, and how to recognize harmful beliefs and change them to constructive ones.

Beliefs: what are they?

Your level of assurance about something is called a belief. That's it. You have a belief about something if you are SURE of its meaning.

Beliefs can be classified as either subconscious or conscious.

Conscious beliefs are those that we are aware of in our minds. We know who they are. You can readily write down someone's instructions on paper if they ask you to. For instance, I can cook well. I'm a good dancer. I'm a decent person.

However, certain beliefs are hidden from our conscious view. We cannot express them, but we can "feel" their impact. Let's examine an illustration. My friend Kamal was naturally expressive when he was with his pals. But if he was at a party or whatever and a few strangers surrounded him, he experienced "fear."

While some people experience mild social anxiety, this was something else entirely. His hands would get sweaty, and his face would turn red. He wanted to leave the place right away since he felt threatened.

After attending therapy sessions for a year, he was able to identify the reason for this phobia. His family attended a sizable funfair when he was a young lad. That funfair drew thousands of visitors.

By accident, he lost his family and became disoriented in the crowd. It was a scary experience for a tiny boy. A tsunami of unidentified persons was coming at him. Some were giving him strange looks. He became even more afraid when some people attempted to communicate with him.

Later, he was located by the security personnel and returned to his family. Although he was unharmed, this terrifying encounter with an unfamiliar person left him with the impression that "strangers are dangerous."

He has held this notion close to his heart, which seriously interfered with his social life. At thirty-two, he was unable to explain WHY he was afraid. All he knew was that he was afraid of social situations.

However, he was able to identify and get rid of the subconscious belief after attending therapy sessions. Your own limiting subconscious beliefs will be discussed later in this chapter.

For now, let's go back to the subject at hand. Everybody has various conscious and subconscious views about various aspects of life.

You still believe in what you deserve out of life, how others are, and who you are. This holds for many aspects of life, including relationships, finances, business, and physical and mental well-being.

Your beliefs in these domains determine your level of success in that specific sector. This holds for everyone, not just you. Our beliefs limit every one of us. According to research, a person's potential for success is determined by where he "believes" his limit.

Take lottery winners who suddenly win big as an example. Even if they might have won a million dollars, they spend it all and return to their pre-lottery state.

Here, we have a strong illustration of limiting belief in action. These individuals always find a way to waste their million dollars and return to their previous state because they subliminally feel they don't deserve it.

"Beliefs create the fact." — William James.

World-renowned experts and trainers like Brian Tracy and Anthony Robbins help you shift your beliefs so they work to your advantage rather than against you.

Positive and negative beliefs are the two categories into which conscious and subconscious beliefs can be divided. Positive beliefs are those that support you in achieving your objectives, whereas negative (or restricting) beliefs are those that prevent you from achieving your goals.

Positive, empowering beliefs that help us achieve our objectives are what we want to replace the negative ones that prevent us from becoming the people we want to be.

It matters because our thoughts influence our actions. If you hold negative thoughts, your mind will constantly generate excuses for why you should give up now rather than try again and why you'll never succeed.

Conversely, having optimistic thoughts will act as an internal coach, encouraging you to keep going despite obstacles.

You are also motivated by your beliefs if you have positive beliefs, that significantly increases your motivation.

Furthermore, the existence of negative ideas HINDERs motivation in the same way that it does action. A pessimistic belief leads you to believe your efforts will ultimately be in vain since you will never accomplish your objective.

As you can see, beliefs are critical to realizing our goal of developing a happy outlook. Our beliefs must support us rather than obstruct our ability to change.

How Did Your Present Beliefs Come To Be?

Most beliefs are created in childhood when the brain is still developing and learning about the outside world's ways. Furthermore, a child's opinions are formed by his environment because it is so unpredictable.

For instance, if a child grows up in a society where money is rare, she will likely develop the mentality that money is hard to get by and scarce. Conversely, a youngster raised in an affluent household may believe wealth is plentiful and accessible.

The randomness of it all is what's surprising. Your environment has the power to shape both your positive and negative views. It is entirely arbitrary.

The good news is that you can alter your beliefs at any time. I had to replace many negative thoughts with positive ones when I began. It had a significant impact on both my level of success and life experiences in general.

Changing might be made much easier if you first modify your beliefs. Permit me to relate a personal story. I received a pair of sunglasses from my older sister when I was a high school student. They looked great on me and were lovely. But I felt I wasn't "cool enough" to wear them, so I didn't wear them to school.

Simply regular sunglasses.

We don't always get what we desire. Our beliefs shape who we are.

Beliefs alter our perspective of reality. Your beliefs are reflected in your reality. They serve as lenses through which we interpret what we see in the outside world. You will see things more positively when you hold optimistic beliefs. It is possible to derive some positive energy from a negative situation.

Negative views will, therefore, cause you to concentrate more on the issues, challenges, and justifications for not even attempting to take action to improve your circumstances.

It's not difficult to identify positive beliefs in those around you if you pay attention. Everybody knows at least a handful of people who are optimistic about the state of the world. These folks have a lot of energy and optimism.

You should try to stay as close to these people as possible because beliefs are CONTAGIOUS, just like feelings. Your perspective will become increasingly optimistic the more time you spend with these people.

Jezebel Spirit Takes Away

This requires you to maintain your course and enjoy God's peace. God never changes; thus, there is still God's peace. He remains the same now as he was yesterday. You may frequently lose concentration and end up losing your freedom. This Spirit is uncontrollable until the word of God is applied to it rather than the individual. You will get God's power when you apply the written word to a given circumstance.

Jezebel Soul Ignores

This ghost rejects authority. It likes to cross boundaries to other roads they are not called to and disobeys people who hold power in the Spirit. I have repeatedly been put to the test by someone who has no fear of God. The guy appeared to get more "out of hand" the more I prayed to God. The devil will stop at nothing to get his hands on your belongings. Many of us would have been consumed by the tail of our lives if it weren't for God's grace. God, however, declares that you are supreme and head. Because favor is within you, it follows you wherever you go and drives demons away. They will remain when you haven't shut the doors and gates of sin that you've opened.

Does Not Send in

This Spirit desires to be in positions of power. Submitting to those in positions of authority is one of a great leader's strongest traits. In business settings, criticism of the organization's head or leader frequently obstructs the organization's mission and strategic goals. Because of this, these executives must have outstanding advisors who won't impede the required advancement. The church is a clear place to witness the Spirit's work. Because a Spirit has frequently stood among them like a god, many great leaders have missed God's will—even God's perfect will. Many pastors, and prophets and apostles in particular, have suffered because of "helpful" advice that pushes them away from God's presence and into regions of vanity. One evening, the Holy Spirit showed me how much he detests arrogance. Even Psalms 18:27, which states, "He will save the afflicted people but will bring down high looks," acknowledges that pride is a sin. One type of disobedience that keeps you from hearing God's voice is pride.

The inability of women, in particular, to submit to their husbands is another way in which this mentality opposes submission. When it yields, it usually does so when it is advantageous or to their liking. God commands us to obey authority and be obedient. You shouldn't be concerned about being popular since it might lead to vanity, particularly if you aren't diligently searching the Bible for revelation.

The Jezebel Spirit Appearing Pure

You will acquire unhealthy habits if you spend enough time with something. If you are not strong enough to live in the shadow of the Almighty, the Spirit will attempt to destroy you based on limiting beliefs and thoughts when you are being taught something. If you don't ask God for assistance in driving out these spirits, no matter how hard you try, only the blood of Jesus Christ can save you. The Spirit arrives early and is highly beneficial. It is sly and crafty in the way it manipulates the brains of its victims using psychological tricks. In reality, the Jezebel Spirit simply considers its interests.

Idols receive the Jezebel Spirit, which guides worship towards them.

The People referred to Paul as God having descended to us in the shape of mankind, according to Acts 14.11–15. This Spirit is given to idols. While receiving compliments and appreciation from others is good, you must never let it replace God. You must never doubt God's ability to deliver you from any situation without requiring you to compromise to advance. Idols are substitutes for the earth, which yearns to be revered, honored, and celebrated. I think you should work as if it were for the Lord. You can cancel any words that are uttered over you with another word. Your blessings will come to you according to what is covering you at any given moment, so you must be continually aware. The Word of God within me is the only reason the Jezebel Spirit, with whom I have come into contact, opposes me. God's word directs your steps, bestows favor, and strengthens you. People are glad to conduct business with me, and I have received a lot of favors because of the word of God. Now that I know how to handle these spirits, I pray to God to help me win my wars. A publisher picked up my self-published book, and it is currently a New York Times Bestseller because God opened the way when you give in to the Holy Ghost's authority over you.

Chapter 2: Step 1: Develop a Realistic and Positive Thought Process

You probably think negatively if you constantly think about the worst-case scenario, bring up your shortcomings, and concentrate on them. Your confidence and sense of self-worth are undermined by negative thoughts, which also prevent you from thinking critically, solving problems effectively, and coming up with new ideas for improving your performance. The first step to changing your thinking is to think realistically and positively. Only then can you practice making decisions and solving problems effectively. Here's how to go about doing it.

Get Rid of the Imposter Feeling

Feeling inadequate and incompetent while reaching your goals and achievements is known as imposter syndrome. You probably have this syndrome if you constantly doubt your talents and have high self-doubt despite your remarkable accomplishments. This is a result of your ongoing self-deprecating behavior as well as your parents' lack of validation and attention during your formative years.

You engage in negative self-talk if you minimize yourself by stating things like "I can't do this," "I will fail again," "I can never win," and similar statements. This causes the "inner critic," a loud, obnoxious voice inside of you, to emerge. Imposter syndrome arises when the inner critic becomes larger and more destructive with time. This syndrome undermines your self-assurance and breeds self-doubt, which makes it harder for you to think optimistically, trust your skills, and make wise judgments. Therefore, to improve your thinking, you must overcome this syndrome.

Start by raising your awareness of your thoughts and record any self-deprecating ideas.

Observe the crippling thought intently and acknowledge its effect on your emotions and behavior.

Right now, just observe it without passing judgment.

Express gratitude to yourself for bringing the concept to your attention, and then consider its veracity.

What evidence do you have to back up your theory if you believe you won't be able to launch and manage your business? What gives you the impression that you are not capable of succeeding? After listing every response you discover, read over the story to confirm that the evidence is accurate and unbiased. You are lying and doubting your abilities if you cannot produce credible evidence. If the belief stems from anything insulting that someone said to you, realize that no one can ever fully know your potential or your hardships in life; as such, you must first believe in yourself.

Now, substitute that harmful suggestion with something more realistically good and repeat the proposal aloud a few times. Change your previous idea to, "I am sure I'll do well if only I work hard and try," if you were thinking, "I am all set up for failure this time, too." To make your recommendations easy to accept and believe, ensure they are positive and grounded in reality.

Chant the idea a few times, and each time it troubles you, make sure you intentionally choose, notice, and transform a negative suggestion into a realistically good one. This teaches you to have an optimistic outlook and cultivate positive beliefs, which will assist you in making wiser judgments.

Develop a "Can Do" mentality.

The set of ideas and convictions that give you the impression that you can do anything and motivate you to make a significant effort in that direction is known as the "can do" mindset. If you don't have a "can do" mentality, you probably give in to your issues whenever they arise. Additionally, it prevents you from operating efficiently and producing the intended outcomes.

To resolve this matter, take the following actions:

Before beginning a significant task or considering a matter and reaching a conclusion, mentally picture it.

Start with the problem and visualize yourself solving it piece by piece with ease.

To interest the viewer, incorporate details into the visualization, such as sights, colors, sounds, and expressions. If you're trying to figure out how to solve the ineffective way that your consumers receive your products, for example, picture yourself as the owner of a delivery system that guarantees effective and efficient delivery to your clients and that your clientele is expanding daily.

Say, "I can do this," and strike a determined attitude, such as a fist pump, while you visualize that situation.

Recite the suggestion aloud a couple more times while grinning and being positive.

Simply identify and carry out the process's initial step. If you need to send an email to a possible investor, for example, write it down and send it after reading it over a few times.

To ensure that you don't put off starting the action, step, activity, or task you want to complete, practice it as soon as you can.

Follow these recommendations religiously to produce fruitful and lasting outcomes quickly.

Establish micro-goals

"You don't have to see the whole staircase; just take the first step," stated Mr. Martin Luther King Jr.

Micro goals are daily objectives you create to achieve your long-term objective. Your micro-objective must be well-defined. Assume, for example, that your macro goal is to have four contacts with whom you may routinely converse about business matters. One such micro-goal would be sending out 20 to 50 emails daily with an introduction to your work and yourself. Your daily to-do list can also be viewed as your micro-goals.

The micro list will help you concentrate on concrete, doable actions to increase self-assurance.

Try to accomplish your objectives for the day, then carry out the same steps the next day. Even if having a big objective is crucial, it could be too much to handle on its own. The process can be initiated by setting a small objective for yourself. Setting and achieving micro-goals is a realistic approach to achieving your goals by requiring consistency. Your sense of achievement will grow if you accomplish your daily micro-goals, which will benefit you. Setting little targets for yourself will help you stay on course and motivate you to keep moving forward. Making a list of micro-goals also makes you prioritize things. You'll create a route map that will assist you in making the essential progress towards your objective. Distractions should be avoided at all costs when working towards micro-goals. For instance, if you send out 20 to 50 emails daily, you must maintain focus and set a deadline. Refuse to use the internet for anything other than emailing people. If you'd like, you can define the objective more precisely, like sending out one to three emails per hour. Reaching micro-goals gives you a sense of success, which improves your attitude. Most critical, though, is that you act.

How To Reduce Your Worry By Being Mindful In The Here And Now

Your life's equilibrium may be impacted by anxiety if you are unable to overcome it. How one escapes this destructive circle is the question. It's easy to find the solution: simply being mindful.

During mindfulness meditation, you focus on your inner.

This chapter discusses mindfulness practices that can help you become worry-free and sharpen your attention in the here and now. Any worry or tension you may be experiencing will be reduced or even eliminated if you only pay attention to the here and now. You will acquire useful skills with scientific support.

Mindfulness: What Is It?

Practicing mindfulness entails being fully aware of your surroundings and focusing both your mental and physical energies on the here and now. It entails being aware of your thoughts and emotions as they arise and developing the ability to observe them without giving them mental space.

There are numerous ways to cultivate awareness, such as mindful eating, attentive breathing, and thoughtful nature walks. Being conscious of your actions at any given time is essential to participating in and living in the present.

How Do Overthinking and Mindfulness Relate to Each Other?

"How does mindfulness help with excessive thinking?" one might wonder. This solution requires a thorough comprehension of what overthinking entails. Individuals overthink because they unknowingly become fixated on a particular concept. You lose awareness of the present and the reality of your surroundings when you give in to worry, fear, or regret.

Because mindfulness allows you to become aware of your ideas and sensations as they arise, it is the ideal treatment for overthinking. In this manner, you can overcome your tendency to let them overwhelm you. By teaching you to notice your thoughts objectively and without bias or attachment, mindfulness helps you resist the pull of your inner voice. It also enables you to become more perspective- and thought-clear. Even when you find yourself sucked into an overthinking pattern, you can identify it.

In what ways, then, may mindfulness help with overthinking?

Here are just a few benefits you will experience:

Decreased Stress and Anxiety

The hormone cortisol, which the body releases in times of stress, can lead to several health issues, including immune system weakness, high blood pressure, and weight gain. But you may lessen your body's release of cortisol by practicing mindfulness, eventually leading to a happy and healthy life.

You may stop the loop of worry and ruminating that ultimately results in overthinking by observing your ideas without becoming attached or passing judgment.

Enhanced Self-Recognition

Being mindful can help you become aware of your behaviors and ideas and identify instances in which you start to overthink situations. You can quickly escape the loop and adopt an optimistic outlook by practicing mindfulness.

Boosts the Respiratory System

Engaging in mindfulness meditation reduces your susceptibility to sickness and ailments. To combat infections, your body produces more killer cells when it experiences less stress and worry.

Enhanced Focus and Attention

When you practice mindfulness and remain present, your ability to focus and concentrate on the activities will increase.

Increased Emotional Hardiness

strength and resilience in the face of difficult circumstances by practicing mindfulness. You can develop the ability to identify uncomfortable you.

Better Quality Sleep

Overanalyzing can prevent you from getting enough. Conversely, mindfulness reduces the negative effects of overthinking on your sleeping patterns by assisting you in de-stressing and winding down before bed.

The study conducted by Amber Hubbling and three colleagues at the University of Minnesota's College of Pharmacy was published in BMC Complementary and Alternative Medicine in 2014.

Their research demonstrated the effects of mindfulness training on adult chronic insomnia through yoga and meditation. They discovered that test subjects' awareness of their thoughts and emotions rose with mindfulness training. Eighteen persons who had completed an 8-week mindfulness training program participated in the study. They were then split into groups and asked to discuss their experiences.

The participants attested that using mindfulness practices improved the quality of their sleep and assisted them in managing their insomnia problems. Additionally, they saw that the individuals' capacity to manage insomnia and sleep quality had improved. The participants stated that practicing mindfulness had positive effects on their bodies as well as their emotions. The group sessions were motivational to them as well.

Based on those findings, the researchers hypothesized that those suffering from chronic insomnia would benefit from mindfulness training and good sleeping practices.

Engaging in Mindfulness Practices

Your obligations to your family, work, relationships, and other commitments can be extremely taxing, and they may even cause you worry and stress. On the other hand, mindfulness training works well for managing stress, reducing overthinking and anxiety, and achieving inner calm and clarity.

Conscious Breathing

The practice of mindful breathing is focusing on and watching your breath without passing judgment. It's a meditation that helps you stay present, mindful, and peaceful. It can also help you declutter, feel better, and experience less tension and anxiety.

In 2016, Hyunju Cho of Yeungnam University in Gyeongsan-si, South Korea's Department of Psychology, released an article on Plos One about the benefits of mindful breathing.

The benefits of mindful breathing exercises regularly, and the researchers examined their efficacy in reducing anxiety in college students. The study had 36 students in total, who were split up into groups. To reduce anxiety, the first group engaged in mindfulness breathing techniques; the second group engaged in a different form of exercise.

Conversely, the third group refrained from engaging in any physical activity. The students were instructed to record their experiences daily throughout the experiment, which lasted roughly six days. Additionally, pre- and post-training questionnaires were given to them to assess how anxious they felt.

The findings showed that alternate workouts and mindful breathing techniques decreased students' anxiety. Additionally, compared to the other groups, those who engaged in mindful breathing exercises reported thinking more positively. These results imply that regular mindful breathing exercises might reduce anxiety and encourage optimistic thinking.

To practice mindfulness breathing, simply follow these easy instructions:

- Locate a cozy chair or cushion to settle onto. If you'd like, you could even lie down.

- Close your eyes and take a few deep breaths to help you relax. Focus on your breathing and pay attention to how your breath feels coming in and out of your nose. Observe how the air feels heated upon exhalation and cool upon inhalation.

- You can focus better by counting your breaths. As you inhale and exhale, count from 1 to 10, then restart at 10.

● When you first start practicing mindful breathing, you may notice your mind wandering to unimportant things. When this occurs, accept the thought and gently return your focus to your breathing instead of trying to suppress it. It's normal to be distracted or to have those ideas, so don't feel bad about it.

● Consistent practice is necessary to become proficient in mindful breathing. Every day, give it a try for five to ten minutes. As you get more comfortable, you can extend the time.

Section 2. Knowing the Law of Attraction

Do you know what the Law of Attraction is? Although this idea has been more well-known recently, its origins can be found in early philosophical teachings. In short, the Law of Attraction says that whatever we focus on, good or bad, that's what we draw into our lives.

This implies that we will draw bad situations into our lives if we are always preoccupied with thinking and believing bad things. On the other hand, we will attract good experiences if we concentrate on having positive thoughts and beliefs. It's crucial to understand that the Law of Attraction is a tool that, when applied correctly, leads a happy life rather than a miraculous panacea.

We must first comprehend the idea of energy to comprehend the Law of Attraction. Energy makes up everything in the universe, including our feelings and thoughts. We release a particular kind of energy when we think or feel anything. We frequently find ourselves surrounded by people and events that are consistent with our feelings and beliefs because this energy attracts other comparable energies.

This energy is the foundation for the Law of Attraction's operation. Our energy is directed toward our desires and goals when we have strong desires or goals. This energy draws other like-minded energies, which advances us toward our goal. But when we doubt ourselves or hold unfavorable thoughts about our capacity to succeed, we release unfavorable energy that can hinder us.

To put it simply, intention, belief, and manifestation are the three main ways the Law of Attraction operates. We draw the tools and opportunities we need to make our goals come true when we have a clear, defined aim and have faith in our ability to accomplish them.

Making our ideas and goals come true is known as manifestation. When we manifest anything, we bring the required energy and resources to make it a reality by directing our thoughts and feelings toward our objective.

It's crucial to remember, though, that manifestation takes time. A desired result requires patience, persistence, and time to materialize. Maintaining your optimism and faith in the process is also critical, especially in the face of seemingly unforeseen circumstances.

Awareness is one of the keys to comprehending and applying the Law of Attraction. Being present at the moment, without distraction or judgment, is the practice of mindfulness. Being mindful makes us more conscious of our feelings and ideas, enabling us to identify and alter harmful habits.

Being thankful for what we have causes us to radiate happiness, which draws additional blessings into our lives.

Regularly practicing thankfulness can assist us in drawing attention to the good things in our lives and helping us attract additional things for which we are thankful.

It is visualization, which goes well with mindfulness and appreciation. Making a mental picture of what we wish to create and concentrating on it with uplifting feelings and ideas is the process of visualization. By putting our ideal result into visual form, we generate a strong energy that draws the tools and circumstances we need to make it happen.

In conclusion, the Law of Attraction is an effective strategy for drawing favorable circumstances and realizing our goals. We may use the Law of Attraction to our advantage and live better, more fulfilled lives by practicing mindfulness and appreciation, using visualization techniques, and comprehending the power of intention, belief, and manifestation.

Get to Know The Most Significant Living Individual

Presenting the principal surviving person!

You will meet him somewhere in this book; it will come as a sudden, unexpected, and heart-stopping acknowledgment that will always alter your life. You will discover his secret nature when you finally meet him. You'll see he wears the initials PMA on one side and NMA on the other to transmit an undetected charm.

This subtle charm possesses two incredible powers: it can attract wealth, success, good fortune, and good health, or it can work against you, depriving you of all that makes life's ordinary experiences worthwhile. A select few guys can rise to the top and stay there thanks to the first of these powers, PMA. The latter is what keeps many guys stationed at the base for the entirety of their lives. When they reach the top, NMA is the one who pulls various men down.

Perhaps S. B. Fuller's account will explain how it works.

Born to a Black sharecropper in Louisiana. "We are poor - not due to God." He started working at the age of five. He was riding donkeys when he was nine years old. Regarding that, it was the same old thing: most residents' children left early for employment. These families accepted poverty as part of their lot in life and didn't expect anything more.

One thing set youthful Fuller apart from his friends: he had an incredible mother. Even though it was all his mother had ever known, she refused to accept this vocal presence for her children. She realized that her family was barely getting along in a world of plenty and delight and that something wasn't quite right. She discussed her fantasies with her child.

She used to say, "S.B., we shouldn't be poor." "What's more never allowed me to hear you say that it is God's Will that we be poor. We are poor - not on account of God. We are poor since father never fostered the craving to get rich. Nobody in our family wants to be something different."

No one genuinely desired wealth. For as long as he can remember, this idea has been ingrained in Fuller so deeply that it has altered. He felt the need to become wealthy. He maintained focus on the necessities and non-necessities in his life. Thus, he encouraged a strong desire to become wealthy. He decided that selling anything would be the fastest way to get money. He selected the cleaner. He took a while to offer it from house to house. Then, he learned the company that had given him would have been sold at a sell-off. The reasonable price was $150,000. He had saved $25,000 in twelve years of selling and putting every penny aside. Everyone agreed he would pay $25,000 and receive the $125,000 excess in ten days. The agreement stated that he would forfeit his store if he failed to collect the money.

In his twelve years as a sales representative for Cleaner, S. B. Fuller was well-liked and respected by many financial experts. Now, he went to them.

He also received financial support from close friends, credit agencies, and investment groups. By the evening of the ninth day, he had amassed $115,000 in funds. He lacked $10,000.

Consider as the light. "I had spent each wellspring of credit I knew," he says. It was late, maybe nightfall. I knelt in the darkness of my chamber and asked God to guide me to someone who could provide the...

$10,000 ahead of time. I promised myself that I would follow 61st Street until I came to the main light in a business foundation, and I prayed for God to use that light as a symbol of His answer."

It was eleven o'clock at night. Whenever S. B. Fuller was driving on 61st Street in Chicago. After a few squares, he finally noticed a light in the office of a worker for hire.

He walked right in. A man Fuller knew was sitting in his work area, a little exhausted after working through the night. Fuller realized he had to be tough.

Fuller asked bluntly, "Need to make $1,000?"

The question alarmed the project worker. "Yes," he said. "Normally."

"Then, at that point, make a check for $10,000, and assuming I bring the cash back, I'll bring back another $1,000 in benefits," Fuller advises this individual. He gave the hired worker the names of the people who had given him money and explained exactly what needed to be done.

How about we look at his enigmatic achievement? Before his departure, S. B. Fuller had a ten thousand dollar check in his pocket that night. By then, he had acquired a larger portion of that company and seven others, including a paper, a hosiery company, a mark company, and four organizations that sold beauty care items. When we recently asked him to join us in discovering the secret to his success, he responded in line with his mother's statement from many years ago:

"We are impoverished—not in God's eyes." Our father never encouraged our desire to become wealthy, so we are impoverished. No one in our family aspires to be someone they're not."

"You see," he explained, "I knew exactly what I needed, but I had no idea how to get it." I read the Bible and books that make a strong argument. I prayed to God for the knowledge I needed to achieve my goals. Three books played a major role in turning my intense desire into reality. They were: (1) the Bible,

(2) Ponder and amass wealth; and (3) The enigma of ages. Reading the Bible is what motivates me the most.

"Assuming that you know what you need, you're bound to remember it when you see it. For instance, when you read a book, you perceive potential chances to get what you need."

S. B. Fuller used the initials PMA on one side and NMA on the other to illustrate the subtle appeal. When he increased the PMA side, amazing things happened. He could bring ideas that previously only existed in his imagination to reality.

Here, it's important to remember that S.B. Compared to most of us, Fuller had fewer privileges at birth. But he chose a big goal and went all out for it. Of course, the target's decision was made by a human. You truly have the right, in this day and age and in this nation, to declare, "This is what I choose. This is what I most need to accomplish." You can achieve your goal unless it violates social norms or the commandments of God. Everything is yours.

To obtain and nothing to lose by making an effort. Individuals who persist in their PMA attempts achieve and maintain success.

What you try will rely on you. Not everyone may like to work for large creation organizations as an SB Fuller. Not everyone would choose to pay the high price of being a master craftsman. The richness of life is very different for certain people. Achievement is one skill in daily life that contributes to a happy, loving life. You, too, can possess these and other forms of wealth. It's up to you to decide.

Nevertheless, it doesn't matter if your definition of success includes:

Being wealthy, as it did for SB Fuller.

Discovering a new scientific component.

Creating music.

Cultivating a rose.

Raising a child.

Find out how success impacts you; the subtle charm featuring the initials PMA on one side and NMA on the other will help you attain it. You can attract the wonderful and lovely using PMA. NMA makes them resentful.

Every challenge has an initial, comparable, or more noticeable advantage. "Be that as it may, imagine a scenario where I have an actual incapacity. What might a difference in mentality do for me?" you could ask. Perhaps the story of Tom Dempsey, a disabled child, can provide you with the answer.

Tom was born with only the stump of his right arm and missing most of his right foot. He had to play sports as a child, just like the other young men. He wanted to be a football player. His parents had an artificial foot created for him because of this wish. It had a wooden construction. The foot made of wood was wearing a rough football boot.

Tom was practicing his wooden foot kicks with the ball hourly at night. He was going to keep trying to score field goals at ever-greater distances. It turned out that he was talented enough to work for the New Orleans Saints.

Around the country, 66,910 football fans could be heard yelling as Tom Dempsey finished the game with two seconds remaining.

- with his crippled leg - kicked a 63-yard field goal to break the record. It was the longest field goal ever scored in a professional football game. The Saints defeated the Detroit Lions 19–17 after that.

Getting Past Obstacles And Adversity

Accepting Change as a Chance for Improvement

Everybody experiences unpredictable and difficult periods in life, which can make us feel helpless and unmotivated. Nevertheless, these are the moments when we can find our inner strength and rekindle our inner fire. Accepting change as a chance for personal development is a philosophy that can improve our lives and help us succeed.

Life will inevitably include change. It can take many forms, such as an abrupt change in circumstances, a personal loss, or a career transition. Although change can be unpleasant and difficult, it offers us amazing opportunities to develop and improve ourselves. We create opportunities and experiences for ourselves when we accept change instead of fighting it.

It is normal to feel overwhelmed and discouraged during trying times. But it's crucial to improvement. We can discover the will to never give up by changing how we think about challenges and seeing them as opportunities rather than barriers.

Developing a growth mindset is one of the keys to accepting change. Failures should not be interpreted as personal failings but rather as insightful lessons that advance our career and personal growth. A growth mindsetallows us to view obstacles as temporary and have faith in our capacity to grow, adapt, and conquer any problem that stands in our way.

Furthermore, we must surround ourselves with a network of supporting people who share our objectives and desires. We can gain encouragement and inspiration from their tales of tenacity and achievement by establishing connections with those who have surmounted comparable obstacles. With cooperation and encouragement, we can get through difficult times with redoubled will and fortitude.

Although change can be unnerving, it presents a chance for introspection and personal development. Accepting change as a chance for development allows us to reach our full potential and find the will and fortitude to get through any hardship. Recall that our future is shaped by how we handle difficult situations, not by them. We can feed the fire within and come out stronger, smarter, and more driven than ever if we have the correct attitude and network of support.

Building Resilience Despite Difficulties

Life is not always easy; it might overwhelm and discourage us because it is full of challenges and hurdles. But it's precisely at these trying times that our ability to bounce back is truly tested. In the book "Fueling the Fire Within: Discovering Motivation for Success," we explore the transforming potential of resilience and how it can be fostered to overcome any hardship in the subchapter "Developing Resilience in the Face of Obstacles."

Fundamentally, resilience is the capacity to overcome obstacles, adjust, and flourish in the face of difficulty. It is a skill that can be acquired over time rather than a quality that some people are born with, and others lack. Nurturing our resilience is crucial to keep going and never give up when life throws challenges.

Shifting our mentality is one of the first steps in developing resilience.

We need to adopt a growth mindset that sees problems as opportunities for learning and growth rather than impassable barriers. We give ourselves the ability to overcome obstacles and develop innovative solutions by changing how we see the world.

Becoming resilient. Having supportive, like-minded people around us who have faith in our skills can inspire us and drive us to keep moving forward. We can get important insights and coping mechanisms to get through difficult times by talking about our troubles and asking people who have faced similar obstacles for advice.

Moreover, self-care and resilience go hand in hand. It is crucial to develop the inner fortitude needed to overcome challenges head-on. Resilience development requires us to prioritize our needs, practice self-reflection and awareness, and partake in joyful activities.

Finally, it is important to recognize and celebrate tiny accomplishments along the way. No matter how tiny, acknowledging and appreciating our accomplishments keeps us motivated and strengthens our resilience. Every advancement, no matter how small, shows that we can overcome challenges and succeed.

The subchapter "Developing Resilience in the Face of Obstacles" is a source of inspiration and hope for people going through difficult circumstances. By embracing a development mentality, establishing a support network, engaging in self-care, and acknowledging accomplishments, an individual can develop resilience, which is a steadfast source of power when confronting life's challenges. Never forget that no matter your challenges, the fire within you can propel you toward victory.

The Biology of Positive Thoughts (Chapter 1)

Your brain will automatically form many negative connections if you think bad thoughts; on the other hand, it will naturally form many positive connections if you only think positively.

The formation and function of neurons, neural pathways, and synapses are determined by the information received; if you feed your mind bad information, your brain will assist you in staying on course negative.

It's true that learning and repetition cause our brains to either remove or build connections.

Our brains start to connect, learn, develop, and alter the instant we are born.

You will always be able to learn, develop, and change—that is until the day you pass away. We are aware that repetition is key to learning.

Consider this: you acquired your first smartphone and had to practice using it repeatedly. Repetition is a favorite brain food.

We only need to know that the more we repeat something, the more the brain learns; there's no need to go into detail on how the brain uses repetition to develop, learn, and change.

From a biological perspective, our minds work best when we repeat what we say and do. Learn, create new connections, and dissolve old ones.

We are fortunate that neuroplasticity allows us to "think" our way into changing our beliefs, mental habits, and actions.

Our minds form connections both consciously and subconsciously in response to external stimuli and to learn. We must intentionally "think" about the material we learn since doing so allows us to foster strong relationships.

Repeating negative ideas and words causes the subconscious to accept them as true, activating the autonomous nervous system.

This is why we never forget how to use our phone, write our name, or ride a bike. These actions are so frequently performed that they come naturally. The same holds for associations and thoughts that are bad.

Repeating positive thoughts repeatedly has the same effect on the brain. When describing oneself, always use uplifting, encouraging, and loving words since your brain will repeat these affirmations more often than negative ones. Although it seems too easy to be true, it is.

Youngsters pick up social and physical skills through direct observation of their parents and firsthand experience. Even if we learn firsthand, our experiences are filtered through the lessons we have received from our parents.

Although no two people have the same upbringing or experiences, we may all acquire the knowledge to create a core belief from repeated negative or positive reinforcement through firsthand experience and parental engagement.

When we were younger, we integrated our experiences into our learning process and moved on without "rationalizing" them. As adults, we can make sense of our experiences, extracting the information we desire and discarding the rest.

Despite our ability to reason and think by ourselves now, we still rely on the experiences we had as children since, throughout that time, our brains were developing rapidly, absorbing everything and creating a vast network of neural connections.

Knowing that the brain processes information from all of our senses, interactions, and activities—and that we can filter that information by thinking and reflecting on our thoughts.

The knowledge we retain and the information we reject can and will change when we consider the causes of our negative attitudes and actions.

Your brain will concentrate more on the good things in your environment and within you, the more positive associations you make. Strong linkages can exist between positive and negative things.

Although our brains tend to focus more quickly on negative associations than on positive ones, we can alter the biology of our brains by creating positive associations and inhibiting negative ones.

How to Create Favorable Connections

Stay conscious of your surroundings and notice the good things about the people and places you are in.

Stay present and devote some effort to finding something positive in the people and surroundings around you.

Describe the good traits you observe in other people.

Exercise because it causes the brain to release hormones that reduce stress; consider the health benefits and emotional lift that exercise provides.

Once you create good brain associations, you will notice virtually instantaneous improvements in your thoughts and emotions.

Positive associations are strengthened when you act positively, and others do the same.

Practice smiling. It may sound ridiculous, but if you grin deliberately, most people will smile back, giving you positive reinforcement.

Easy Reminders

The brain can adapt, expand, and learn until the day of death.

Examine the causes of your pessimistic thoughts.

Repetition of uplifting associations and ideas

Maintain your attention in the here and now.

The Beneficial Effects of Positive Thought on Physical Health

Physicians know that thinking positively significantly influences healing, recuperation times, and pain thresholds.

Before surgery, people who approach the procedure with optimism recover more quickly than those who don't.

Remarkably, optimists are less likely to get sick and have better immune systems than pessimists.

Positive emotions also cause certain biochemical alterations in the person experiencing them, and the opposite is equally true for negative or traumatic emotions.

A broken heart can hurt physically in the chest; blood vessels constrict, and arrhythmias have been known to occur in some situations.

Individuals who feel love receive an additional opioid boost from their bodies, which contrasts sharply with the physical symptoms of a shattered heart.

Hugging, kissing, and affectionate physical contact cause the body to release oxytocin, a naturally occurring opioid, as its name implies.

When moms and infants come into physical contact, oxytocin is released. This release of oxytocin strengthens their bond. Breastfeeding causes mothers to release oxytocin, which calms and soothes both mother and infant. The brain is trained to repeat the action that caused the release of oxytocin as a reward.

Pleasure is experienced when feel-good chemicals are released into our bloodstream, and this pleasure guarantees that we will repeat the acts that caused the release.

Feel-good chemicals are also released in response to positive ideas. The interaction between the body's innate behavioral programming and positive thoughts and feelings.

When the mother can hold and touch her child, the infant in the NICU does better. The mother's physical touch soothes the baby and lessens tension for both parties.

The power of good action and attitude is demonstrated by the subtle but evident benefits a woman and her infant in the NICU experience both mentally and physically.

www.ingramcontent.com/pod-product-compliance
Lightning Source LLC
Chambersburg PA
CBHW052135110526
44591CB00012B/1725